My Cozy Blanket of Air

Brrrr! It's freezing outside! But I'm warm inside my layers of clothes. I'm wearing two shirts and a sweater under my coat. I'm also wearing a blanket of air.

My blanket of air is under my coat. It is made of air trapped between my clothes. Even the little holes that dot my sweater and hat hold air! The air slows my body's heat from getting out of my clothes and keeps me cozy.

See how fluffy and soft that bird looks? It has puffed up its feathers to keep warm. The puffed feathers trap air and hold it close to the bird's body. The air insulates the bird. It helps keep out the cold and hold in the heat.

I have fluffy feathers, too! They are inside my coat. These fluffy feathers are called down. Down traps lots of air. It is a good insulator.

I find the tracks of mice. The mice run and sleep in tunnels beneath the snow. Snow is full of air, so it works like the down in my coat. It helps keep the mice a little warmer on a very cold day.

I go inside when I start to shiver. I look out my window. It is made of two panes of glass with a layer of air between them. The air slows the heat from leaving the house through the window, and it helps keep the cold from creeping in.

I snuggle under my quilt at night. It is stuffed with fluffy feathers just like my coat is. I stay toasty all through the cold winter night under my quilt—and my blanket of air.